Build Your Own VPN
A Step by Step Guide

Copyright © 2023 Lin Song. All Rights Reserved.

ISBN 979-8987508923

No part of this publication may be reproduced, stored or transmitted in any form or by any means, electronic, mechanical, photocopying, recording, scanning, or otherwise without written permission from the author. It is illegal to copy this book, post it to a website, or distribute it by any other means without permission.

Designations used by companies to distinguish their products are often claimed as trademarks. All brand names and product names used in this book and on its cover are trade names, service marks, trademarks and registered trademarks of their respective owners. The author and the book are not associated with any product or vendor mentioned in this book. None of the companies referenced within the book have endorsed the book.

Although the author has made every effort to ensure that the information in this book was correct at press time, the author does not assume and hereby disclaims any liability to any party for any loss, damage, or disruption caused by errors or omissions, whether such errors or omissions result from negligence, accident, or any other cause.

Table of Contents

1 Introduction
    1.1 Why build your own VPN
    1.2 About this book
2 Create a Cloud Server
    2.1 Create a server on DigitalOcean
    2.2 Create a server on Vultr
    2.3 Create a server on Linode
    2.4 Create a server on OVH
3 Set Up the VPN Server
    3.1 Connect to the server using SSH
    3.2 Update the server
    3.3 Install WireGuard
    3.4 Install OpenVPN
    3.5 Install IPsec VPN with IKEv2
4 Configure VPN Clients
    4.1 Transfer files from the server
    4.2 Configure WireGuard VPN clients
        4.2.1 Windows
        4.2.2 macOS
        4.2.3 Android
        4.2.4 iOS (iPhone/iPad)
    4.3 Configure OpenVPN clients
        4.3.1 Windows
        4.3.2 macOS
        4.3.3 Android
        4.3.4 iOS (iPhone/iPad)
    4.4 Configure IKEv2 VPN clients
        4.4.1 Windows
        4.4.2 macOS

- 4.4.3 Android
- 4.4.4 iOS (iPhone/iPad)
- 4.4.5 Chrome OS (Chromebook)

5 Manage VPN Clients
- 5.1 Manage WireGuard VPN clients
  - 5.1.1 Add a new client
  - 5.1.2 List existing clients
  - 5.1.3 Remove a client
- 5.2 Manage OpenVPN clients
  - 5.2.1 Add a new client
  - 5.2.2 Export an existing client
  - 5.2.3 List existing clients
  - 5.2.4 Revoke a client
- 5.3 Manage IKEv2 VPN clients
  - 5.3.1 Add a new client
  - 5.3.2 Export an existing client
  - 5.3.3 List existing clients
  - 5.3.4 Revoke a client
  - 5.3.5 Delete a client

About the Author

1 Introduction

1.1 Why build your own VPN

In today's digital age, online privacy and security have become increasingly important. Hackers and other malicious actors are constantly looking for ways to steal personal information and sensitive data, making it essential to take necessary measures to safeguard our online activities.

One way to enhance online privacy and security is by building your own virtual private network (VPN), which can offer a range of benefits:

1. Increased privacy: By building your own VPN, you can ensure that your internet traffic is encrypted and hidden from prying eyes, such as your internet service provider. Using a VPN can be especially useful while utilizing unsecured Wi-Fi networks, such as those found in coffee shops, airports, or hotel rooms. It can help protect your online activities and personal data from being tracked, monitored, or intercepted.

2. Greater security: Public VPN services can be vulnerable to hacks and data breaches, which can expose your personal information to cybercriminals. By building your own VPN, you can have greater control over the security of your connection and the data that is transmitted over it.

3. Access to geographically-restricted content: Some websites and online services may be restricted in certain regions, but by connecting to a VPN server located in another region, you may be able to access content that is otherwise unavailable to you.

4. Cost-effective: While there are many public VPN services available, most of them require a subscription fee. By building your own VPN, you can avoid these costs and have more control over your VPN usage.

5. Flexibility and customization: Building your own VPN allows you to customize your VPN experience according to your specific needs. You can choose the level of encryption you want to use, the location of the server, and the network protocol such as TCP or UDP. This flexibility can help you optimize your VPN for specific activities such as gaming, streaming, or downloading, providing a seamless and secure experience.

Overall, building your own VPN can be an effective way to enhance online privacy and security while also providing flexibility and cost-effectiveness. With the right resources and guidance, it can be a valuable investment in your online security.

1.2 About this book

This book is a step-by-step guide to building your own IPsec VPN, OpenVPN and WireGuard server. In Chapter 2, you will learn how to create a cloud server on providers such as DigitalOcean, Vultr, Linode and OVH. Chapter 3 covers connecting to the server using SSH and setting up WireGuard,

OpenVPN and IPsec VPN. Chapter 4 covers VPN client setup on Windows, macOS, Android and iOS. In Chapter 5, you will learn how to manage VPN clients.

IPsec VPN, OpenVPN and WireGuard are popular and widely used VPN protocols. Internet Protocol Security (IPsec) is a secure network protocol suite. OpenVPN is an open-source, robust and highly flexible VPN protocol. WireGuard is a fast and modern VPN designed with the goals of ease of use and high performance.

2 Create a Cloud Server

As a first step, you will need a cloud server or virtual private server (VPS) to build your own VPN. For your reference, here are some popular server providers:

- DigitalOcean (https://www.digitalocean.com)
- Vultr (https://www.vultr.com)
- Linode (https://www.linode.com)
- OVH (https://www.ovhcloud.com/en/vps/)

First, choose a server provider. Then refer to the example steps in this chapter to get started. When creating your server, it is recommended to select the latest Ubuntu Linux LTS or Debian Linux (Ubuntu 22.04 or Debian 12 at the time of writing) as the operating system, with 1 GB or more memory (RAM).

Advanced users can set up the VPN server on a Raspberry Pi. First log into your Raspberry Pi, then follow the instructions in Chapter 3, Set Up the VPN Server. Before connecting, you may need to forward port(s) on your router to the Raspberry Pi's local IP. Refer to the default ports for each VPN type in Chapter 3.

2.1 Create a server on DigitalOcean

1. Sign up for a DigitalOcean account: Go to the DigitalOcean website (https://www.digitalocean.com) and sign up for an account if you haven't already.

2. Once you're logged in to the DigitalOcean dashboard, click the "Create" button in the top right corner of the screen and select "Droplets" from the dropdown menu.

3. Select a datacenter region based on your requirements, e.g. closest to your location.

4. Under "Choose an image", select the latest Ubuntu Linux LTS version (e.g. Ubuntu 22.04) from the list of available images.

5. Choose a plan for your server. You can select from various options based on your needs. For a personal VPN, a basic shared CPU plan with regular SSD disk and 1 GB memory is likely sufficient.

6. Select "Password" as the authentication method, then enter a strong and secure root password. For your server's security, it is crucial that you choose a strong and secure root password. Alternatively, you may use SSH keys for authentication.

7. Select any additional options such as backups and IPv6 if you want.

8. Enter a hostname for your server and click "Create Droplet".

9. Wait a few minutes for the server to be created.

Once your server is ready, you can log in via SSH using the username `root` and the password you entered when creating the server. See Chapter 3 for more details.

2.2 Create a server on Vultr

1. Sign up for a Vultr account: Go to the Vultr website (https://www.vultr.com) and sign up for an account if you haven't already.

2. Once you're logged in to the Vultr dashboard, click the "+" button and select "Deploy New Server".

3. Choose a plan for your server. You can select from various options based on your needs. For a personal VPN, a cloud compute regular performance plan is likely sufficient.

4. Choose a server location based on your requirements, e.g. closest to your location.

5. Select the latest Ubuntu Linux LTS version (e.g. Ubuntu 22.04) as the server image.

6. Select the desired server size based on your needs. For a personal VPN, 1 GB memory is likely sufficient.

7. Choose any additional options you need, such as backups and IPv6.

8. Enter a server hostname and label.

9. Click on "Deploy Now".

10. Wait a few minutes for the server to be created.

Once your server is ready, you can log in via SSH using the username `root` and the password provided in the Vultr control panel. See Chapter 3 for more details.

2.3 Create a server on Linode

1. Sign up for a Linode account: Go to the Akamai Linode website (https://www.linode.com) and sign up for an account if you haven't already.

2. Once you're logged in to the Akamai Linode dashboard, click on the "Create" button in the top left corner of the screen, then select "Linode" from the dropdown menu.

3. Select the latest Ubuntu Linux LTS version (e.g. Ubuntu 22.04) as the server image.

4. Choose a region where you want your server to be located and select a plan based on your requirements. For a personal VPN, a 1 GB shared CPU plan is likely sufficient.

5. Enter a strong and secure root password for authentication. For your server's security, it is crucial that you choose a strong and secure root password. In addition, you also have the option to use SSH keys for authentication.

6. Select any additional options you need, such as backups.

7. Click on the "Create Linode" button.

8. Wait a few minutes for the server to be created.

Once your server is ready, you can log in via SSH using the username `root` and the password you entered when creating the server. See Chapter 3 for more details.

2.4 Create a server on OVH

1. Go to the OVH VPS website: https://www.ovhcloud.com/en/vps/

2. Choose a plan for your server. For a personal VPN, a "starter" or "value" plan is likely sufficient.

3. Click on the "Order now" button next to the VPS plan you want to use.

4. Select "Distribution only", then select the latest Ubuntu Linux LTS version (e.g. Ubuntu 22.04) as the operating system.

5. Choose the data center location where you want your server to be located.

6. Select any additional options you need, such as snapshots.

7. Review your order, then click on the "Login and pay" button.

8. Log in to your OVH account or create a new account if you don't have one.

9. Confirm your order and make the payment.

10. Wait for your server to be provisioned. This process may take a few minutes.

Once your server is ready, you can log in via SSH using the username `root` and the password provided in your email from OVH. See Chapter 3 for more details.

3 Set Up the VPN Server

After your cloud server or virtual private server (VPS) is created, follow instructions in this chapter to connect to your server using SSH, update the operating system, and install WireGuard, OpenVPN and/or IPsec VPN with IKEv2.

3.1 Connect to the server using SSH

Once your cloud server is created, you can access it via SSH. You can use the terminal on your local computer or a tool like Git for Windows to connect to your server using its IP address and your root login credentials.

To connect to your server using SSH from Windows, macOS or Linux, follow the steps below:

1. Open the terminal on your computer. On Windows, you can use a terminal emulator like Git for Windows.

   Git for Windows: https://git-scm.com/downloads
   Download the portable version, then double-click to install. When finished, open the `PortableGit` folder and double-click to run `git-bash.exe`.

2. Type the following command, replacing `username` with your username (e.g. `root`) and `server-ip` with your server's IP address or hostname:

   `ssh username@server-ip`

9

3. If this is your first time connecting to the server, you may be prompted to accept the server's SSH key fingerprint. Type "yes" and press enter to continue.

4. If you are using a password to log in, you will be prompted to enter your password. Type your password and press enter.

5. If this is your first time connecting to the server, and you are prompted to change the root password, enter a strong and secure new password. Otherwise, skip this step. For your server's security, it is crucial that you choose a strong and secure root password.

6. Once you are authenticated, you will be logged in to the server via SSH.

7. You can now run commands on the server through the terminal.

8. To disconnect from the server, simply type the `exit` command and press enter.

3.2 Update the server

After connecting to the server using SSH, you can update it by running the following commands and reboot. This is optional, but recommended.

```
sudo apt update && sudo apt -y upgrade
sudo reboot
```

Linux server security best practices recommend that you regularly update your server's operating system to keep it up to date with the latest security patches and updates.

3.3 Install WireGuard

GitHub: https://github.com/hwdsl2/wireguard-install

First, connect to your server using SSH.

Download the WireGuard install script:

```
wget https://get.vpnsetup.net/wg -O wg.sh
```

Option 1: Auto install WireGuard using default options.

```
sudo bash wg.sh --auto
```

For servers with an external firewall (e.g. Amazon EC2), open UDP port 51820 for the VPN.

Option 2: Interactive install using custom options.

```
sudo bash wg.sh
```

You can customize the following options: VPN server's DNS name, UDP port, DNS server for VPN clients and name of the first client.

After setup, you can run the script again to manage users or uninstall WireGuard. See Chapter 5 for more details.

Next steps: Get your computer or device to use the VPN. See:

4.2 Configure WireGuard VPN clients

Enjoy your very own VPN!

3.4 Install OpenVPN

GitHub: https://github.com/hwdsl2/openvpn-install

First, connect to your server using SSH.

Download the OpenVPN install script:

```
wget https://get.vpnsetup.net/ovpn -O ovpn.sh
```

Option 1: Auto install OpenVPN using default options.

```
sudo bash ovpn.sh --auto
```

For servers with an external firewall (e.g. Amazon EC2), open UDP port 1194 for the VPN.

Option 2: Interactive install using custom options.

```
sudo bash ovpn.sh
```

You can customize the following options: VPN server's DNS name, protocol (TCP/UDP) and port, DNS server for VPN clients and name of the first client.

After setup, you can run the script again to manage users or uninstall OpenVPN. See Chapter 5 for more details.

Next steps: Get your computer or device to use the VPN. See:

4.3 Configure OpenVPN clients

Enjoy your very own VPN!

3.5 Install IPsec VPN with IKEv2

GitHub: https://github.com/hwdsl2/setup-ipsec-vpn

First, connect to your server using SSH.

Download the IPsec VPN install script:

```
wget https://get.vpnsetup.net -O vpn.sh
```

Option 1: Auto install using default options.

```
sudo sh vpn.sh
```

For servers with an external firewall (e.g. Amazon EC2), open UDP ports 500 and 4500 for the VPN.

Option 2: Interactive install using custom options.

```
sudo VPN_SKIP_IKEV2=yes sh vpn.sh
sudo ikev2.sh
```

After setup, you can run `sudo ikev2.sh` to manage IKEv2 clients. See Chapter 5 for more details.

Next steps: Get your computer or device to use the VPN. See:

4.4 Configure IKEv2 VPN clients

Enjoy your very own VPN!

4 Configure VPN Clients

In this chapter, you will learn how to transfer client configuration file(s) from the VPN server to your local computer, and configure WireGuard, OpenVPN and IKEv2 VPN clients on Windows, macOS, Android and iOS.

4.1 Transfer files from the server

When configuring VPN clients, you may need to securely transfer client configuration file(s) from the server to your local computer. One way to do this is by using the `scp` command. Example steps:

1. Open the terminal on your computer. On Windows, you can use a terminal emulator like Git for Windows.

   Git for Windows: https://git-scm.com/downloads
   Download the portable version, then double-click to install. When finished, open the `PortableGit` folder and double-click to run `git-bash.exe`.

2. Type the following command, replacing `username` with your SSH username (e.g. `root`), `server-ip` with your server's IP address or hostname, `/path/to/file` with the path to the file on the server, and `/local/folder` with the local folder where you want to save the file.

   ```
   scp username@server-ip:/path/to/file /local/folder
   ```

3. For example, if you want to authenticate as `root` and transfer `/root/client.conf` from the server with IP address `192.0.2.1` to the current working folder on the local computer:

   ```
   scp root@192.0.2.1:/root/client.conf ./
   ```

   Note: If using Git for Windows, the local folder `/` usually points to the installation folder, e.g. `PortableGit`.

4. If you are using a password to log in, you will be prompted to enter your password. Type your password and press enter.

5. The file will then be transferred from the server and saved to the local folder you specified.

4.2 Configure WireGuard VPN clients

WireGuard VPN clients are available for Windows, macOS, iOS and Android (https://www.wireguard.com/install/).

To add a VPN connection, open the WireGuard App on your mobile device, tap the "Add" button, then scan the generated QR code in the script output. For Windows and macOS, first securely transfer the generated `.conf` file to your computer, then open WireGuard and import the file.

To manage WireGuard VPN clients, run the install script again: `sudo bash wg.sh`. See Chapter 5 for more details.

- Platforms

- Windows
- macOS
- Android
- iOS (iPhone/iPad)

WireGuard VPN clients: https://www.wireguard.com/install/

4.2.1 Windows

1. Securely transfer the generated `.conf` file to your computer.
2. Install and launch the **WireGuard** VPN client.
3. Click **Import tunnel(s) from file**.
4. Browse to and select the `.conf` file, then click **Open**.
5. Click **Activate**.

4.2.2 macOS

1. Securely transfer the generated `.conf` file to your computer.
2. Install and launch the **WireGuard** App from **App Store**.
3. Click **Import tunnel(s) from file**.
4. Browse to and select the `.conf` file, then click **Open**.
5. Click **Activate**.

4.2.3 Android

1. Install and launch the **WireGuard** App from **Google Play**.
2. Tap the "+" button, then tap **Scan from QR code**.
3. Scan the generated QR code in the output of the VPN script.

4. Enter anything you like for the **Tunnel Name**.
5. Tap **Create tunnel**.
6. Slide the switch ON for the new VPN profile.

4.2.4 iOS (iPhone/iPad)

1. Install and launch the **WireGuard** App from **App Store**.
2. Tap **Add a tunnel**, then tap **Create from QR code**.
3. Scan the generated QR code in the output of the VPN script.
4. Enter anything you like for the tunnel name.
5. Tap **Save**.
6. Slide the switch ON for the new VPN profile.

4.3 Configure OpenVPN clients

OpenVPN clients (https://openvpn.net/vpn-client/) are available for Windows, macOS, iOS and Android. macOS users can also use Tunnelblick (https://tunnelblick.net).

To add a VPN connection, first securely transfer the generated `.ovpn` file to your device, then open the OpenVPN App and import the VPN profile.

To manage OpenVPN clients, run the install script again: `sudo bash ovpn.sh`. See Chapter 5 for more details.

- Platforms
    - Windows
    - macOS
    - Android
    - iOS (iPhone/iPad)

OpenVPN clients: https://openvpn.net/vpn-client/

4.3.1 Windows

1. Securely transfer the generated `.ovpn` file to your computer.
2. Install and launch the **OpenVPN Connect** VPN client.
3. On the **Import Profile** screen, click the **File** tab.
4. Drag and drop the `.ovpn` file into the window, or browse to and select the `.ovpn` file, then click **Open**.
5. Click **Connect**.

4.3.2 macOS

1. Securely transfer the generated `.ovpn` file to your computer.
2. Install and launch Tunnelblick (https://tunnelblick.net).
3. On the welcome screen, click **I have configuration files**.
4. On the **Add a Configuration** screen, click **OK**.
5. Click the Tunnelblick icon in the menu bar, then select **VPN Details**.
6. Drag and drop the `.ovpn` file into the **Configurations** window (left pane).
7. Follow on-screen instructions to install the OpenVPN profile.
8. Click **Connect**.

4.3.3 Android

1. Securely transfer the generated `.ovpn` file to your Android device.

2. Install and launch **OpenVPN Connect** from **Google Play**.
3. On the **Import Profile** screen, tap the **File** tab.
4. Tap **Browse**, then browse to and select the `.ovpn` file.

   Note: To find the `.ovpn` file, tap the three-line menu button, then browse to the location you saved the file.
5. On the **Imported Profile** screen, tap **Add**.
6. Tap the new OpenVPN profile to connect.

4.3.4 iOS (iPhone/iPad)

First, install and launch **OpenVPN Connect** from **App Store**. Then securely transfer the generated `.ovpn` file to your iOS device. To transfer the file, you may use:

1. AirDrop the file and open with OpenVPN, or
2. Upload to your device (OpenVPN App folder) using File Sharing (https://support.apple.com/en-us/HT210598), then launch the OpenVPN Connect App and tap the **File** tab.

When finished, tap **Add** to import the VPN profile, then tap **Connect**.

To customize settings for the OpenVPN Connect App, tap the three-line menu button, then tap **Settings**.

4.4 Configure IKEv2 VPN clients

IKEv2 is natively supported by Windows, macOS, iOS and Chrome OS. There is no additional software to install. Android users can use the free strongSwan VPN client.

To manage IKEv2 clients, run `sudo ikev2.sh` on your server. See Chapter 5 for more details.

- Platforms
    - Windows
    - macOS
    - Android
    - iOS (iPhone/iPad)
    - Chrome OS (Chromebook)

4.4.1 Windows

Screencast: IKEv2 Auto Import Configuration on Windows https://youtu.be/H8-S35Og0eE

Windows 8, 10 and 11 users can automatically import IKEv2 configuration:

1. Securely transfer the generated `.p12` file to your computer.
2. Download ikev2_config_import.cmd (https://github.com/hwdsl2/vpn-extras/releases/latest/download/ikev2_config_import.cmd) and save this helper script to the **same folder** as the `.p12` file.
3. Right-click on the saved script, select **Properties**. Click on **Unblock** at the bottom, then click on **OK**.
4. Right-click on the saved script, select **Run as administrator** and follow the prompts.

To connect to the VPN: Click on the wireless/network icon in your system tray, select the new VPN entry, and click **Connect**. Once connected, you can verify that your traffic is being routed properly by looking up your IP address on Google. It should say "Your public IP address is `Your VPN Server IP`".

4.4.2 macOS

Screencast: IKEv2 Import Configuration and Connect on macOS
https://youtu.be/E2IZMUtR7kU

First, securely transfer the generated `.mobileconfig` file to your Mac, then double-click and follow the prompts to import as a macOS profile. If your Mac runs macOS Big Sur or newer, open System Preferences and go to the Profiles section to finish importing. For macOS Ventura and newer, open System Settings and search for Profiles. When finished, check to make sure "IKEv2 VPN" is listed under System Preferences -> Profiles.

To connect to the VPN:

1. Open System Preferences and go to the Network section.
2. Select the VPN connection with `Your VPN Server IP`.
3. Check the **Show VPN status in menu bar** checkbox. For macOS Ventura and newer, this setting can be configured in System Settings -> Control Center -> Menu Bar Only section.
4. Click **Connect**, or slide the VPN switch ON.

(Optional feature) Enable **VPN On Demand** to automatically start a VPN connection when your Mac is on Wi-Fi. To enable, check the **Connect on demand** checkbox for the VPN connection, and click **Apply**. To find this setting on macOS Ventura and newer, click on the "i" icon on the right of the VPN connection.

Once connected, you can verify that your traffic is being routed properly by looking up your IP address on Google. It should say "Your public IP address is `Your VPN Server IP`".

4.4.3 Android

Screencast: Connect using Android strongSwan VPN Client
https://youtu.be/i6j1N_7cI-w

1. Securely transfer the generated `.sswan` file to your Android device.
2. Install strongSwan VPN Client from **Google Play**.
3. Launch the strongSwan VPN client.
4. Tap the "more options" menu on top right, then tap **Import VPN profile**.
5. Choose the `.sswan` file you transferred from the VPN server.
   Note: To find the `.sswan` file, tap the three-line menu button, then browse to the location you saved the file.
6. On the "Import VPN profile" screen, tap **Import certificate from VPN profile**, and follow the prompts.
7. On the "Choose certificate" screen, select the new client certificate, then tap **Select**.
8. Tap **Import**.
9. Tap the new VPN profile to connect.

(Optional feature) You can choose to enable the "Always-on VPN" feature on Android. Launch the **Settings** app, go to Network & internet -> Advanced -> VPN, click the gear icon on the right of "strongSwan VPN Client", then enable the **Always-on VPN** and **Block connections without VPN** options.

Once connected, you can verify that your traffic is being routed properly by looking up your IP address on Google. It should say "Your public IP address is `Your VPN Server IP`".

4.4.4 iOS (iPhone/iPad)

Screencast: IKEv2 Import Configuration and Connect on iOS (iPhone & iPad)
https://youtube.com/shorts/Y5HuX7jk_Kc

First, securely transfer the generated `.mobileconfig` file to your iOS device, then import it as an iOS profile. To transfer the file, you may use:

1. AirDrop, or
2. Upload to your device (any App folder) using File Sharing (https://support.apple.com/en-us/HT210598), then open the "Files" App on your iOS device, move the uploaded file to the "On My iPhone" folder. After that, tap the file and go to the "Settings" App to import, or
3. Host the file on a secure website of yours, then download and import it in Mobile Safari.

When finished, check to make sure "IKEv2 VPN" is listed under Settings -> General -> VPN & Device Management or Profile(s).

To connect to the VPN:

1. Go to Settings -> VPN. Select the VPN connection with `Your VPN Server IP`.

2. Slide the **VPN** switch ON.

(Optional feature) Enable **VPN On Demand** to automatically start a VPN connection when your iOS device is on Wi-Fi. To enable, tap the "i" icon on the right of the VPN connection, and enable **Connect On Demand**.

Once connected, you can verify that your traffic is being routed properly by looking up your IP address on Google. It should say "Your public IP address is `Your VPN Server IP`".

4.4.5 Chrome OS (Chromebook)

First, on your VPN server, export the CA certificate as `ca.cer`:

```
sudo certutil -L -d sql:/etc/ipsec.d \
  -n "IKEv2 VPN CA" -a -o ca.cer
```

Securely transfer the generated `.p12` and `ca.cer` files to your Chrome OS device.

Install user and CA certificates:

1. Open a new tab in Google Chrome.
2. In the address bar, enter:
   chrome://settings/certificates
3. **(Important)** Click **Import and Bind**, not **Import**.
4. In the box that opens, choose the `.p12` file you transferred from the VPN server and select **Open**.
5. Click **OK** if the certificate does not have a password. Otherwise, enter the certificate's password.
6. Click the **Authorities** tab. Then click **Import**.
7. In the box that opens, select **All files** in the drop-down menu at the bottom left.

8. Choose the `ca.cer` file you transferred from the VPN server and select **Open**.
9. Keep the default options and click **OK**.

Add a new VPN connection:

1. Go to Settings -> Network.
2. Click **Add connection**, then click **Add built-in VPN**.
3. Enter anything you like for the **Service name**.
4. Select **IPsec (IKEv2)** in the **Provider type** drop-down menu.
5. Enter `Your VPN Server IP` for the **Server hostname**.
6. Select **User certificate** in the **Authentication type** drop-down menu.
7. Select **IKEv2 VPN CA [IKEv2 VPN CA]** in the **Server CA certificate** drop-down menu.
8. Select **IKEv2 VPN CA [client name]** in the **User certificate** drop-down menu.
9. Leave other fields blank.
10. Enable **Save identity and password**.
11. Click **Connect**.

(Optional feature) You can choose to enable the "Always-on VPN" feature on Chrome OS. To manage this setting, go to Settings -> Network, then click **VPN**.

Once connected, you will see a VPN icon overlay on the network status icon. You can verify that your traffic is being routed properly by looking up your IP address on Google. It should say "Your public IP address is `Your VPN Server IP`".

5 Manage VPN Clients

After setting up the VPN server, you can manage WireGuard, OpenVPN and IKEv2 VPN clients by following the instructions in this chapter.

For example, you can add new VPN client(s) on the server for your additional computers and mobile devices, list existing VPN clients, or export configuration for an existing client.

5.1 Manage WireGuard VPN clients

To manage WireGuard VPN clients, first connect to your server using SSH (see Chapter 3), then run:

```
sudo bash wg.sh
```

You will see the following options:

```
WireGuard is already installed.

Select an option:
  1) Add a new client
  2) List existing clients
  3) Remove an existing client
  4) Remove WireGuard
  5) Exit
Option:
```

You can then enter your desired option to add, list or remove WireGuard VPN client(s).

Note: These options may change in newer versions of the script. Read carefully before selecting your desired option.

5.1.1 Add a new client

To add a new WireGuard VPN client:

1. Select option 1 from the menu, by typing 1 and pressing enter.
2. Provide a name for the new client.
3. Select a DNS server for the new client, which will be used while connected to the VPN.

Next steps: Configure WireGuard VPN clients. See Chapter 4, section 4.2 for more details.

5.1.2 List existing clients

Select option 2 from the menu, by typing 2 and pressing enter. The script will then display a list of existing WireGuard VPN clients.

5.1.3 Remove a client

To remove an existing WireGuard VPN client:

1. Select option 3 from the menu, by typing 3 and pressing enter.
2. From the list of existing clients, select the client you want to remove.
3. Confirm the client removal.

5.2 Manage OpenVPN clients

To manage OpenVPN clients, first connect to your server using SSH (see Chapter 3), then run:

```
sudo bash ovpn.sh
```

You will see the following options:

```
OpenVPN is already installed.

Select an option:
 1) Add a new client
 2) Export config for an existing client
 3) List existing clients
 4) Revoke an existing client
 5) Remove OpenVPN
 6) Exit
Option:
```

You can then enter your desired option to add, export, list or revoke OpenVPN client(s).

Note: These options may change in newer versions of the script. Read carefully before selecting your desired option.

5.2.1 Add a new client

To add a new OpenVPN client:

1. Select option 1 from the menu, by typing 1 and pressing enter.
2. Provide a name for the new client.

Next steps: Configure OpenVPN clients. See Chapter 4, section 4.3 for more details.

5.2.2 Export an existing client

To export OpenVPN configuration for an existing client:

1. Select option 2 from the menu, by typing 2 and pressing enter.
2. From the list of existing clients, select the client you want to export.

5.2.3 List existing clients

Select option 3 from the menu, by typing 3 and pressing enter. The script will then display a list of existing OpenVPN clients.

5.2.4 Revoke a client

In certain circumstances, you may need to revoke a previously generated OpenVPN client certificate.

1. Select option 4 from the menu, by typing 4 and pressing enter.
2. From the list of existing clients, select the client you want to revoke.
3. Confirm the client revocation.

5.3 Manage IKEv2 VPN clients

To manage IKEv2 VPN clients, first connect to your server using SSH (see Chapter 3), then run:

```
sudo ikev2.sh
```

You will see the following options:

```
IKEv2 is already set up on this server.

Select an option:
  1) Add a new client
  2) Export config for an existing client
  3) List existing clients
  4) Revoke an existing client
  5) Delete an existing client
  6) Remove IKEv2
  7) Exit
Option:
```

You can then enter your desired option to manage IKEv2 clients.

Note: These options may change in newer versions of the script. Read carefully before selecting your desired option.

Alternatively, you may run `ikev2.sh` with command-line options. See below for details.

5.3.1 Add a new client

To add a new IKEv2 client:

1. Select option 1 from the menu, by typing 1 and pressing enter.
2. Provide a name for the new client.
3. Specify the validity period for the new client certificate.

Alternatively, you may run `ikev2.sh` with the `--addclient` option. Use option -h to show usage.

```
sudo ikev2.sh --addclient [client name]
```

Next steps: Configure IKEv2 VPN clients. See Chapter 4, section 4.4 for more details.

5.3.2 Export an existing client

To export IKEv2 configuration for an existing client:

1. Select option 2 from the menu, by typing 2 and pressing enter.
2. From the list of existing clients, enter the name of the client you want to export.

Alternatively, you may run `ikev2.sh` with the `--exportclient` option.

```
sudo ikev2.sh --exportclient [client name]
```

5.3.3 List existing clients

Select option 3 from the menu, by typing 3 and pressing enter. The script will then display a list of existing IKEv2 clients.

Alternatively, you may run `ikev2.sh` with the `--listclients` option.

```
sudo ikev2.sh --listclients
```

5.3.4 Revoke a client

In certain circumstances, you may need to revoke a previously generated IKEv2 client certificate.

1. Select option 4 from the menu, by typing 4 and pressing enter.
2. From the list of existing clients, enter the name of the client you want to revoke.
3. Confirm the client revocation.

Alternatively, you may run `ikev2.sh` with the `--revokeclient` option.

```
sudo ikev2.sh --revokeclient [client name]
```

5.3.5 Delete a client

To delete an existing IKEv2 client:

1. Select option 5 from the menu, by typing 5 and pressing enter.
2. From the list of existing clients, enter the name of the client you want to delete.
3. Confirm the client deletion.

Alternatively, you may run `ikev2.sh` with the `--deleteclient` option.

```
sudo ikev2.sh --deleteclient [client name]
```

About the Author

Lin Song, PhD, is a Software Engineer and open source developer. He created and maintains the Setup IPsec VPN projects on GitHub since 2014, for building your own VPN server in just a few minutes. The projects have 20,000+ GitHub stars and 30 million+ Docker pulls, and have helped millions of users set up their own VPN servers.

Connect with Lin Song
GitHub: https://github.com/hwdsl2
LinkedIn: https://www.linkedin.com/in/linsongui

Thanks for reading! I do hope you get the best from reading this book. If this book was helpful to you, I'd be very grateful if you leave a rating or post a short review.

Thanks,
Lin Song
Author

Printed in Great Britain
by Amazon